THE BOOK RACK
1933 Fruitville Pike
Lancaster, PA
581-5887

400

Selling Price _____

That Day
In
September

That Day In September

written by Artie Van Why

Van Hughes Publishing
New York, NY - Lancaster, PA
(In association with Lulu Press)

® Writers Guild of America 2005

Library of Congress Registration No. PAu-2-706-968

PRINTED IN THE UNITED STATES OF AMERICA
BY LULU PRESS

First paperback edition published 2006

ISBN 978-1-4116-8315-0

For my parents, Art and Thelma Van Why

Acknowledgments

In thanking the people who have contributed professionally and/or personally to the evolution of *That Day In September,* I have to mention first, and foremost, Richard Masur. It was with his help that my words began to take form as a script. Richard encouraged me in the writing of it...committed himself to the directing of it...and supported me throughout the whole process.

Secondly, I have to thank James Carey for giving me the first opportunity to bring my words alive on stage at California Lutheran University and at the Celebration Theatre in Los Angeles.

I want to thank Carolyn Rossi Copeland, at the Lambs' Theatre, for allowing me to achieve my dream of telling my story Off Broadway in New York.

On a more personal side, there are many people to thank. It would be impossible to mention everyone. Throughout the months of writing, it was the people of New But West that were a source of continued support. They reminded me to take it one day at a time. And there was always the support of friends, to which I will be forever grateful.

I owe a great deal of thanks to Christine Cetrangelo, who was there to help in whatever way needed. And I will always be grateful for James Harder, being there throughout.

Thanks, and appreciation, for my family, who have always been there for me.

And last, but certainly not the least, is Ronald H. Hughes, to whom I owe so much, both professionally and personally. If not for him, this book wouldn't have happened.

Dedicated to the lives lost

From the Author

We all have our stories to tell about where we were the morning of September 11, 2001. Whether in New York City or miles away, we all witnessed, and were part of, the horror of that day. Whether we watched the events unfold personally or on television, we were all affected, and changed, by that day.

This just happens to be my story...no more important or significant than yours. Just from my perspective. My experience. Along with your own memories of 9/11, perhaps these words will give you an added insight as to what it was like to be present in New York City on that morning...and the weeks and months following.

I live with the memory of 9/11 still...to this very day, often questioning why I survived, while others didn't. I live each day wishing there was more I could have done that morning.

The one thing I can do now is to continue to tell my story...to help keep the memory of that day alive. To honor those who died. That is my sole desire. To let my words be just a small piece of the history of that day in September.

Thank you for letting me share my story with you.

Artie Van Why

Reflection

I want it to go away. I don't want it to have happened.

But it won't, and it did, and I was there.

I wanted to catch that falling man with the flailing arms and legs.

But I couldn't, and I didn't, though I was there.

I wanted to be a hero, doing more than I humanly could.

But I wasn't, and I didn't.

I wanted to stay there, in the street, not afraid.

But I didn't, and I was.

I wanted to be there through the end.

But I wasn't.

I wanted to stay and rescue.

But I didn't.

I wanted to be more injured, more dirty, more at risk.

But I wasn't.

I want to imagine being buried, being missing, being gone.

But I can't.

I want to know why I survived, and others didn't.

But I don't.

I want it never to have happened.

But it did.

A Loud Boom

I don't remember which came first, the shudder of the building or the loud sound. They probably came at the same time.

I don't remember how long it took before someone ran into the word processing center where I worked and told us that a plane had hit one of the World Trade Center towers. It seemed like seconds but was probably at least a minute or two.

In whatever the order, there was a loud boom; our building shook, and then there was quiet. My coworkers and I looked at one another.

I remember saying, "What was that?" Someone else asked, "Was that thunder?" What it had sounded like to me was as if a huge, metal trash dumpster had been dropped onto the 24th floor above me. That would have explained the reverberations of the building I had felt, but I knew there was no construction going on up there. Had something possibly exploded?

Someone ran into the center and told us that a secretary, who had just come to work, was hysterical, saying that a plane had hit one of the towers and that it was like a war zone out there. One of our phones rang, and it was our supervisor, calling from home. She screamed to the person who answered something about seeing it on TV and for us to, "Get out of the building!"

What? My initial reaction was to go downstairs and see what was going on—more out of curiosity than alarm. I went to the elevator bank, along with a few other people who had the same idea. As we descended, though I didn't consciously think it through, I know I assumed a light plane had smashed into the tower. I imagined a small hole in the building, with the back end of a plane sticking out. Our conversation, as we headed down from the 23rd floor, was tinged with nervousness, but not fear. When the elevator doors opened to our lobby, I took a quick right and walked through a side revolving door.

As I passed through that door and out onto the street, three things went through my mind. The secretary was right; it did look like a war zone. It also looked like a movie set...for a disaster film. And it was like going through the door in *The Wizard of Oz*, walking out into a world that was unlike anything that I could ever have possibly imagined.

My Life Before

I moved to New York in November 1977. Actually, to be more specific, I was brought to New York in November 1977. Brought by a woman and remained because of an incredibly lucky encounter.

The year before, I had graduated from a small, conservative Christian college down south. A scholastically liberal arts environment with no drinking, swearing, smoking, dancing, long hair, blue jeans or public displays of affection. Yes…I went there on my own volition. I had become involved in the "Jesus Movement" my senior year of high school (it was big in the early seventies). It even made the cover of *Time* or *Newsweek*—not my conversion, but the movement itself.

Anyway, believing I had a "calling," I entered, my freshman year, as a Bible major, with the sincere intention of pursuing a religious life. I was ready to discover all the mysteries that would be revealed to me.

My junior year I had two revelations that I wasn't quite prepared for. I realized, one, that I wanted to be an actor—and, two, that I was gay. I don't know which of those discoveries was more upsetting. Or which came first. To be honest, though, they were actually two things I had known about myself since early childhood. The acting had been discouraged because it wasn't a "realistic, practical goal" (or so I was told). And as for the other thing, I knew, even as a child, that when I said I wanted to go and play with the boys, I wasn't thinking baseball. And I had gotten the message that that was definitely something "not to talk about."

So here are these two things about myself I had to face. Something had to be done. After much turmoil, thought, prayer and meditation, I "came out"…I declared myself a Drama major. I decided to keep quiet (and stay in) about the, uh, other thing.

So, I became the big fish in our very small pond of a Drama Department. A Drama Department where all scripts had to be reviewed, edited and approved before being presented, and where, though we put on musicals, they were done, of course, without the choreography. No dancing, remember? It was not the best of institutes to learn the craft of acting.

As to my sexual identity, I went through those last two years of college never talking to anyone about it. They didn't ask, and I didn't tell. And I always thought I was the "only one." It wasn't till years later that I found out that really wasn't true. But that's another story.

After graduating with a B.A. in Drama, I went back to my hometown in Maryland to live with my family while deciding what to do next with my life and my degree. With my B.A. in hand, I naturally went to work as a shipping clerk for a pharmaceutical company. That was by day. By night, I performed in community theater. And by day AND night, I did my best not to be asked, and not to tell, about "the other thing," thinking if I ignored it, it would go away.

My big break came when I was cast in the title role of a professional dinner theater production of *Norman, Is That You?* (a comedy about a young gay man who's terrified to come out of the closet). I didn't have a clue.

It was because of this role, in this play, that I ended up in New York. Not in the way you might think. I developed a close friendship with one of the women in the show. Let's call her "Karen." Having had no substantial emotional ties (or physical ties or sexual ties or any other kind of ties) with any other woman up till that time, I jumped…no, I grabbed onto the idea that I was in love with Karen and therefore normal. I had confessed to her, at the start of our relationship, that I thought I was gay, but didn't want to be. In spite of that admission, Karen declared she, too, was in love. And, she also had a little admission of her own. She already had a boyfriend in New York.

After our last performance, the week before Thanksgiving, that November of 1977, Karen and I got in my car and drove to New York. I was taking her there so she could spend some time with the boyfriend. Me? I would get to visit New York for two days. I would then just go back to Maryland and wait for her to decide whom she wanted to be with.

She had arranged to sublet a studio apartment for herself, so I would stay there with her for the two days I was to be in New York. We drove in on a Monday night. I'll never forget driving in on the NJ Turnpike and seeing the lights of the city's skyline for the first time.

The next day, our first full day in the city I saw my first Broadway show: *A Chorus Line*. Now *that* was an introduction to New York theater and Broadway. Wednesday, which was to be my last day with her and with the city, Karen asked how I wanted to spend it. See the Empire State Building maybe, or the World Trade Center, or maybe, just spend the day with her. My choice was to see Liza Minnelli in *The Act*. And I still didn't have a clue.

Anyway, it was while killing time before that Wednesday matinee that I had the incredibly lucky encounter. I ran into someone I knew from college. He had moved to the city the year before. After the usual "I can't believe we ran into each other" (already an example of how small this big city is), he told me that he was on break from rehearsing a new show, and that one of their actors had dropped out that morning. A replacement was needed right away.

Well, in true show biz story fashion, he took me to meet the director, and whether because of my limitless talent, or their desperation, they offered me the role. Liza and a part in a New York show in the same afternoon. Could it get any better?

I drove back to Maryland that night, gave my parents my car, and took the train back to my new home and my new career as a New York actor. In a matter of weeks, I was making my New York debut working a very large puppet on a stick in a Christmas play for children.

I soon dropped the stick, after that show, and began to get real roles, in real plays.

Karen, the woman I brought up to New York, broke up with the boyfriend, and she and I continued to share that small studio sublet. It was in the West Village, near Christopher Street, and for some reason I really loved it down there. I was beginning to get a clue.

I was living the life of the "struggling actor," and I couldn't have been happier, but it wasn't too long before I realized I was also living the life of the "struggling-closeted-gay-man-living-with-his-girlfriend," and I couldn't have been more confused. One life in public. Another life in secret, trying to deny, while trying to find out, just who I was. And all of this within my first six months of living in New York.

It took a number of years for me to come to grips with myself, and my sexuality. They were difficult years, far too long to go into here. But, in a nutshell, I slowly opened that closet I had kept myself in for so long. I came out to those around me. The climax of that process being my coming out to my sister and two very accepting parents.

And Karen? The woman for, and with whom, I had traveled to New York? She has a full life—married, with children, and very happy.

By my tenth year in the city, my dreams of becoming a star had been "downsized" to hopes of just making a living as an actor, but even those redefined hopes had pretty much faded away. I was hardly pursuing my acting by that point. My income was now exclusively from temp jobs. Through those temp jobs, I had taught myself word processing and, by then, had become pretty good at it. I found myself with a marketable skill now that seemed more useful than any talent I might have.

I don't think there was a specific day when I decided to finally give up acting, but one day, I went to an employment agency. "Just to see." My first offer of a job came with the first interview I was sent out on. A "real" job with a steady paycheck, benefits and paid vacations. I accepted the job, making a promise to myself that it would only be for a year or two. I would get some money in the bank and then go back to my acting career or decide on something else to do.

Well, that year or two stretched into three or four. Then four and more. So, I had given up acting…and taken up drinking.

I worked as the sole word processor on the evening shift at a midsize law firm in midtown Manhattan. My hours were from five to midnight. That was fine with me…and great for my social life.

Most of my friends, at that time, were still actors themselves (meaning most of them were waiters), and they worked hours similar to mine. In essence, our "evenings" started at midnight, and what better place to begin them but at a bar.

A rut is easy to fall into. And I fell into one that was pretty deep, pretty "wet" and not very pretty.

There comes a time for some of us, I guess, when the subtle awareness of the question "how did I get here?" grows into a harsh reality. As long as I could remember, from my imagination as a child, through my daydreams of adolescence, past my expectations of young adulthood, I know I had never pictured that some day I would be in a career I hadn't chosen, in a job that wasn't fulfilling, paying off debts that never ended, being alone way too often, and drinking way more than I needed, wanted or was good for me.

I wanted more out of life; that was for sure. But the hope I tried to hold onto was the false hope that my life would change on its own. Somewhere, there would be "a right place" to be at "the right time" where I'd run into "the right person" that would magically change my life.

So pour me a drink and let me complain about what could have been. Pour me another and I'll tell you my thoughts on what should have been. And with "one for the road," I'll give you a few hindsight observations on what would have been. Coulda, shoulda, woulda.

And that was pretty much my life…for about ten years. No magic…just that.

In January 1999, much to my surprise, I finally had that moment of being in the right place, at the right time, with the right person. The place was my apartment; the time was one hung-over morning, and the person was me. I decided I had to do something. I had to get sober. Little did I know that I had taken the first step towards "not only living without drinking, but also living" period. So I did what I had to. I got sober.

With the help of the twelve steps, a group of loving, caring recovering alcoholics that I became a part of, and with the awareness of a power greater than myself, my life began to change. I began to change.

As "one day at a time" went by, the days became weeks, the weeks turned into months, and those months had quickly become two years. I was staying sober. And along with sobriety came clarity—about myself, about my life. And out of clarity grew self-respect, and the belief that life was now something to embrace, not hide from.

For too long, I had lived my life as if it were something to be endured, not explored. I was unearthing the sense of hope that had long been covered by fear. The fear of failure. Of not "getting it right." I had allowed discouragement to become despair. With that newfound hope, I rediscovered the goals that had long been ignored and the dreams that had been dashed by disappointments.

For once, I felt entitled to fulfillment, to happiness, to living life "beyond my wildest dreams." I simply started to want more for my life. It seemed daring to want to be happy.

I allowed myself to question choices I had made. Those life choices I had made, or rather had let life's circumstances and situations make for me.

One of those biggest choices had been my life's work. As for my career, I had long ago stopped looking for what I wanted, settling for what I thought I needed, or should need.

Perhaps it was time to ask myself what it was I truly wanted. What it was I wanted to be doing. Time to look at whatever gifts or talents I might have; time to believe it was okay to want to use them.

The habits of living life one way are not that easily broken. I wasn't yet ready, or prepared, to take leaps into the new and unknown. But I entered our new century believing change was possible.

In the beginning of 2001, a rumor began to spread around work that our law firm was going to either close up shop or merge with a larger firm. After months of speculation and second-guessing on the staff's part, it was announced that, at the end of May, the firm was merging with a big law firm downtown. And even though this was a job I'd been trying to figure out how to leave, I was just as anxious as everyone else about whether or not I'd still have my job after the merger.

As it turned out, they wanted me to work in the word processing center of the new firm, where I would now be working with three others, on a regular daytime shift—8:30 in the morning to 4:30 in the afternoon. I was given just a few days to decide if I wanted to accept the offer. So, ironically, now that my initial fears were eased, and I knew I still had a job, I was at the proverbial fork in the road, and I was more scared than ever. On the one hand, I could stick with a job that offered a steady paycheck. On the other hand, maybe this was an opportunity to examine some of those dreams that I had filed under "I can't" or "It wouldn't work."

It was like being on the edge of a cliff, looking out at the expanse of possibilities before me. Could I take what would have to be a "leap of faith," and turn down the job and just jump out into the unknown? That would be a huge leap.

So, at the end of May, my midsize law firm packed up, closed its doors, and, on June 1, 2001, merged with the other firm and moved to their offices downtown—across from the World Trade Center...and I went with them.

Out Onto the Street

As I passed through the revolving door and out onto the street, it was like stepping into a snowstorm. Everything was white. The sidewalks and the streets—as far as I could see—were covered with what looked like a surreal blanket of fresh fallen snow. Paper of all sorts and sizes was scattered everywhere, coming down from the sky all around me, like bizarre flakes. There were whole sheets of paper and scraps of paper and bits of paper floating down from as far up as I could see. I had never seen so much paper.

I took the few steps that brought me to Church Street. I stood in front of the World Trade Center, between the Millennium Hotel and the Century 21 store. I noticed other objects and forms and substances on the ground—clumps of insulation, chunks of what looked like plasterboard. My attention left the ground though, as, with those few steps toward Church Street, my head tilted upward, finally letting the north tower become my focus. Oh my God! What was supposed to have been just a small hole made by a little plane was a huge canyon blasted into the side of the tower. Smoke, the thickest and blackest I've ever seen, billowed from the gaping wound. Flames of the brightest oranges and reds shot out from the blackness.

I know that, in the back of my mind, the thought that people were dead had to be registering, but right then, I couldn't get past just staring at the destruction and thinking about how bad it looked.

The sound of sirens seemed to be coming from everywhere. The surrounding buildings were starting to evacuate, and the streets were filling up with people. Behind me, a crowd already had gathered, everyone doing as I was, staring at the burning, smoking north tower. Large pieces of debris were falling down the length of the tower. One of the pieces of falling debris seemed to be moving. It was moving, and it wasn't debris. It was a person falling, arms and legs waving madly. A woman behind me screamed. I, and others, screamed with her as more and more people began jumping from the tower.

NO!

A Glorious Summer

I fell in love with the World Trade Center my first week down there. Oh, I had certainly been down there a few times before in all my years of living in New York, usually as a tour guide for friends or family who happened to be visiting. Then, all I thought it was about was going to the observation deck. I had no idea those Twin Towers and all that was below them and all that surrounded them were like a city within the city.

I adapted quickly to working days; that was no problem. Since I had become sober, I had discovered the pleasure of rising early. I loved getting downtown each day and soon developed a daily routine. I'd be coming up onto the street, out of the subway, by 8 a.m. If it wasn't raining (which I don't remember it doing much during those months), I'd walk the few blocks to the World Trade Center. The streets were always dotted with the familiar sight of shiny aluminum carts, with just enough space for a person to stand inside and serve coffee, bagels, and assorted pastries. My first morning, I stopped at one, and I went to the same cart, on the same corner, across from Building Number 5, every morning, including September 11th.

I didn't know his name, and he didn't know mine, but the man in that cart became my "coffee man." Within my first week, he had memorized how I liked my coffee, which I think he tried to do for all his regular customers. Every day he greeted me with a "good morning, my friend" and had my large coffee, half regular, half decaf, skim milk, Sweet'N Low™ on the side, ready for me by the time I got my dollar out. If I happened to miss stopping by on any given morning, he'd ask me where I had been the next time he saw me. That only happens in this city.

I'd sit each morning on one of the stone-slab benches that were around the perimeter of the fountain at the World Trade Center with a copy of the newspaper I had picked up. I would read my paper, drink my coffee, smoke a cigarette. I would watch the people passing me on their way to work.

Often during that morning ritual of mine, I felt reassured that life was good. When the weather was favorable, the sky a bright blue, and the summer breeze light and warm, it always seemed that all was right with the world in those quiet minutes alone. Just as it did that morning in September.

If the weather was bad, there was the massive shopping mall below those looming towers—a perfect refuge and ideal place to pass extra time. There was the spectrum of stores and shops to look through and all those places to get something to eat. I also spent many a lunch hour in the bookstore in Building Number 5, flipping through a magazine, looking for that next good book to read, or listening to CDs in the music section.

But, my favorite thing to do at lunchtime, if the weather permitted, was to sit in that expansive plaza area watched over by not only the towers but also the other buildings that made up the World Trade Center. It was summer, and summer at the World Trade Center was glorious. At lunchtime the plaza would be filled with people and activity—vendors selling hot dogs or ice cream or pretzels; people who were part of the community of workers would eat their lunches (brought from home or bought from there); the men would have their suit jackets off, their ties loosened, and top shirt buttons undone; the women, in their business attire, would be sitting with their shoes kicked off. People would be getting a head start on their tans, sitting within and around the plaza area, heads tilted back, facing the sun, getting those few important minutes of "sun time."

There were the tourists, identifiable by the inevitable cameras around their necks or in their hands. Though they're easy targets to poke fun at, they're the ones who reminded me of the magic of this city, seeing in their expressions and hearing in their exclamations the astonishment of what they were experiencing all around them.

Then there was the fountain, balancing the sculpture of a sphere atop it. A stylized globe made of different color metals. It was right in the middle of the plaza, circled by one continuous bench. I often sat there, my own face up to the sun, listening to the soft sound of the water spilling over into the fountain's bottom. If I closed my eyes, I could pretend I was near an ocean's shore—very relaxing.

During the summer months, there were free noontime concerts in the plaza. Rows of folding chairs faced a temporary stage of steel and metal. Each day a specific style of music was performed live: jazz, country, bebop, doo-wop or my favorite—"golden oldies" day. Here I'd be, in the middle of New York, in the middle of my workday, listening to Peter Noone of Herman's Hermits one day, Mark Lindsay of Paul Revere and the Raiders on another. On those days in particular, the "golden oldies" days, people would get up out of their folding chairs and dance in front of the stage or right where they were—an elderly couple here, two female coworkers laughing while dancing over there—the maintenance man, the businessman, the young secretary, everyone forgetting they would soon be heading back to work—and, oh yes, the tourists smiling for the picture being taken of them dancing away.

Perhaps I idealize it, now that it's gone, but I don't think so. It was an oasis for the worker in a tedious workday, a fascination for the visitor seeing the sights, a small world of its own that held some of the elements that make New York so dynamic, so interesting, and oh so alive.

It had a breath of its own.

The War Zone

No! No! No!

One person after another plunged down the length of the North Tower, alongside pieces of wreckage from the plane and the tower. Why were they jumping? I wanted to stop them. To stop this awful reality. I wanted each "No" that I screamed to stop each person from hitting the ground. I wanted my shouts to push them back up to where they had jumped from. No, I wanted to help them. I started running toward the plaza, running past the stone benches I used to sit on. Past a photographer quickly snapping pictures. I ran through that blizzard of falling paper, knowing I had to help those people. I could now see much larger objects were falling in the plaza. Out of the corner of my eye, I saw a man following behind me on my right.

I bolted up the plaza steps and stopped at the southwest corner of Building Number 5, under the protection of an overhang. The north tower was right across from me, less than a block away. It loomed upward; the only thing separating me from the tower was a section of the plaza, where huge pieces of twisted metal shapes were crashing onto the concrete, each impact booming thunderously. Large shards of glass from blown out windows fell steadily, sounding like a hard hailstorm as piece after piece hit the ground, shattering. I wanted to run across the plaza toward the tower, but there was all that debris falling. Frantically looking around, I saw that the overhang I stood under went along the length of Building Number 5, and I thought maybe I could run around to the tower, protected by it, and be able to get closer to the people on the ground. Maybe I could pull someone to safety that might still be alive. Hold someone's hand until help came.

Just as I started to move, my attention was broken when something caught my eye, and I looked up and to my left, and saw another man falling. But this time, much closer, and with much greater detail. I couldn't take my eyes off him, and as he neared the ground, I saw clearly how frantically his arms and legs were moving, as if he was desperately trying to slow himself down. As I was about to see him hit the ground, his descent took him behind the stage where I had watched those noontime concerts.

The man who had been running behind me from my right reached me and stopped. I turned to ask, "What do we do?" and was aware of someone falling on top of a pile of clothes just across the plaza. It took an instant to register that it wasn't a pile of clothes. The person had fallen on top of a pile of bodies that were already lying there. I stood and stared as one body after another fell.

And the bodies and debris kept falling and falling until shouts from two guards drew my attention to a side entrance of Building Number 5, where they were holding the door open and screaming for us to get in. One last, quick look at the intensity of wreckage and people falling told us we had no choice. If we wanted to live, we had to run toward the two guards. We ran into Building Number 5 and joined a crowd of other people evacuating the building. We went out a front entrance right next to my favorite bookstore. I pushed through the crowded streets and sidewalks to get back to where I had been standing on Church Street, feeling I needed to get back there, to that exact spot, though I don't know why. Whatever the reasons, I was only standing there for a brief moment before the others and I heard the incredibly loud sound of an airplane, the second plane, as it approached the south tower. Looking up, and to my left, the plane was so big, and so close to the top of the buildings it passed. I stared at the plane not believing it would hit the tower.

The middle floors of the tower blew outward in a massive inferno of bright orange flames and dense clouds of black smoke. Time stood still for just a second, as if we all were suspended in disbelief. In the next beat, pandemonium broke out. Screaming, panic, mass confusion. I, along with everyone in the street, just started running, literally running for our lives. Twisted metal, glass and other debris were raining down on us. I ran towards Fulton Street, thinking, at one point, that I was going to run right out of the loafers I was wearing. As I turned east onto Fulton, I slipped, and fell to my hands and knees. Some people stepped on top of me, pushing me to the ground, and I thought, for one brief moment, that I was going to be trampled to death. But I got back on my feet, started running, and stepped on someone, myself. I remember running and saying out loud, "God save us all."

To my right, I saw a man scrambling to get under a van. He was dressed in a suit and was lying on his back, desperately trying to slither beneath the protection of the vehicle. I remember glancing at his face, and our eyes locked for one brief second. The look of sheer terror on his face was so contorted that I almost laughed out loud. I don't know why I didn't.

Up ahead of me, a man was lying in the middle of Fulton Street. He was a heavyset man in a suit, lying on his stomach. Everyone was running right by him. I started to run past him myself, but for whatever reason, I stopped and ran over to him. I dropped to my knees at his side. It was then I noticed all the blood and where it was coming from. His skull had been split open, and the top part of his brain was protruding through the split. Blood was gushing out of the wound. Amazingly, he was breathing. I saw, lying near his head, a putty knife—a regular looking putty knife that had an almost even line of blood on its blade. I thought, oh my God, is this what hit him? I remember putting it back down as another man came running over, dropping down on his knees on the other side. Someone handed a denim jacket to me saying "take this." I took it and applied it over the opening in his skull. The other man who had come over put his hand on top of mine, and we held the jacket there with all the pressure we could summon, trying desperately to slow down the flow of blood. Now that the falling debris had lessened people were stopping and others ran over to us. An ambulance was on Church Street. We all started screaming for it. "Over here! Over here!"

As the ambulance began to make its way toward us, through the debris in the street, someone, who said they knew first aid, suggested we turn the man over onto his back. Four of us did so, carefully. His teeth were covered with blood and dirt or soot or something, and two of us used our fingers to clean out his mouth. I noticed that his watch was lying there beside him, having come off. I picked it up and put it in his left pants' pocket. His employee work tag was hanging around his neck. I didn't really look at it. I wish, now, that I had. I wish that I had looked at his name and memorized it, so I could find his family and tell them that he wasn't alone, that he had people with him.

The ambulance reached us, and a flat board was brought over. He was so big it took at least six of us to gingerly get him onto it. He was belted to the board, and we lifted him and carried him to the back of the ambulance. I remember touching his arm and whispering to him, "You'll be okay. You'll be okay."

As the ambulance began maneuvering up Fulton Street, I followed it up to Broadway. I looked at my hands and saw that they were covered with the man's blood. There was another ambulance on Broadway, already treating some of those with minor injuries. I went up to one of the EMS workers and just showed her my hands. At first, she thought it was coming from me, but I told her, "No…it's someone else's." She had me sit down on the curb and said she would be right over to wash my hands. A man in a suit looked down at me and asked if I was okay. He was the only person who asked me that all day. The EMS worker returned, knelt in front of me, and began cleaning my hands. I looked right at her. "What's going on?" I remember her looking at me and saying, "I don't know, but this is awful."

She helped me up from the curb and went to attend to others. I was in front of my office building, and I saw one of my coworkers. I went up to her, and we hugged. She later told me I was shaking like a leaf.

I suddenly thought of my parents seeing all this on TV. I started going up to people, asking, "Can I use your cell phone?"—but none of them were working. The lines at the pay phones were already very long, so I started walking north asking anyone I saw with a cell phone if their phone was working. Some were, some weren't, but no one would let me make my call.

Finally, I darted into a coffee shop that was empty except for a few of its workers. There was a man behind the counter. I screamed, "Can I use your phone?" In a daze, he motioned towards the back. I could only remember one number, and it was a friend who worked uptown. Amazingly I got through to him and simply yelled into the phone, "Billy, it's Artie. Call my parents. I can't remember their number. Van Why. In Millersville, or Lancaster, Pennsylvania. Tell them I'm okay. Okay?" I hung up.

I walked out of the coffee shop, which was about 10 blocks north of the towers. It was then that the south tower collapsed, sounding like yet another explosion. In frenzied confusion, everyone looked at one another, not knowing what was happening. In panic, we all just started running. I looked behind me and saw this huge wall of debris, dust and smoke rapidly moving toward me. "What in God's name was happening?" People were screaming, some crying hysterically. I kept running until I couldn't run anymore. Eventually, I slowed down, gasping for breath. I then began the long walk home, to midtown Manhattan, along with everyone else. In absolute silence.

An Obvious Stillness

There was an obvious stillness in the air as the hordes of us walked, dazed and shocked, uptown. Thousands of us. Strangers. A mass of silent humanity walking together.

I remember seeing a woman's high-heel shoe, lying in the street, and wondering if she was still walking with just one shoe on.

Getting closer to midtown, I noticed people on the street corners gathered around radios. I began hearing whispers of "the Pentagon" and "Pennsylvania."

I, like almost everyone else, instinctively started veering west as we neared midtown, veering away from the Empire State Building.

It was about 12:45 when I finally arrived at my apartment. I saw that my answering machine was blinking with, I don't remember how many, messages. I sat down on my bed and tried to think of what to do next. At some point, I looked down and saw that I had put a pair of shorts on. I don't remember doing that. Then I saw that both of my knees were scraped and had been bleeding. I ignored them, trying to think of what to do next. Every circuit in my brain was on overload; anxiety, images and thoughts were running rampant. I needed to get out of my apartment. But then what? As if a life preserver were thrown, I remembered the noontime twelve-step meeting in my neighborhood that I had gone to every weekday before my firm moved downtown. I would go there. Leaving my apartment building, I began walking over to the church in Times Square where the meeting was held each day.

The meeting was at its midpoint. The turnout was much smaller than usual, the mood much more somber. I heard a woman say, just as I walked in, "I'm worried about the people I know who work down there." She saw me enter and said, "But one of them just walked in." All eyes were on me as I took a seat. I raised my hand to speak. I began sobbing, trying to find the words to describe what I had witnessed. There was a man I didn't know sitting to my left. I remember he was wearing a white chef's jacket. He brought his chair closer to me and put his arm around me. When I could speak no longer, he kept his arm around me for the remainder of the meeting. As soon as it ended, others came over to me, hugging me, holding me. In a way, I felt safely "at home."

One of the men walked me home, stopping at his apartment to get something I hadn't thought of. He got bandages for my knees.

When I returned to my apartment after the meeting, I listened to the messages on my machine. Call after call from friends, relatives, people I hadn't heard from in years, all asking the same question: "Are you okay?" The only people I remember speaking to that night were my sister and my parents.

The Next Morning

Walking out onto the street the next morning was like walking into stillness. There were no cars on the streets, no horns blaring. Only the occasional wail of a siren haunted the quiet. I remember the weather being, as it was the day before, beautiful.

I had slept very little. I had slept with a light on.

It was early, about 7:00 in the morning. I couldn't put the television on. I had tried to watch a bit of the coverage the previous evening, but I had to turn it off. I couldn't watch one more replay of the towers being struck, of people falling, of buildings collapsing. My personal experience was enough. I didn't need other people's images. I didn't turn my television on for weeks and weeks, until the nonstop coverage had ceased. And even then, the moment a newsbreak or story came on about the aftermath of the terrorist attack, I turned off the set.

I couldn't look at or read a newspaper. I didn't need to be reminded in print of what had taken place. I couldn't look at front pages, couldn't read headlines. The first time I did buy a paper after the 11th, I turned a page at one point only to see a picture of a man, in midair, stopped by the camera as he fell from the north tower.

Mornings were the hardest for me. For everyone in New York, probably. There would be that one brief second when waking up, where the mind was still a bit unfocused. That brief second of disconnection from the real world. In an instant, though, reality pushed its way to the forefront. The images and sounds of that awful morning flooding back into my thoughts.

I couldn't stay inside my apartment the morning of the 12th. I needed to be outside; I needed to see other people. My routine most mornings, when waking up, was to go across the street to a small outdoor café, to get my first cup of coffee for the day. It was familiar, and it was what I knew. It's what I did that morning. Crossing the street, I didn't know if it would be open, but it was. The owner, a woman, was standing in the middle of the café, with, what would become common among us all, a look of aftershock. I thanked her for being open. She replied that she felt she "had to do something." She unnecessarily apologized because there would be no morning delivery of fresh baked goods. She took what pastries and bagels she had left from the previous day and, along with large thermal urns of coffee, set up a table just outside of the café, near the small tables. She didn't charge for any of it that morning. What she had was offered for free, to anyone who came by hoping to find the place open. I sat at one of the tables, drinking my coffee. Other people, some of them recognizable regulars, began coming by. Each person remarked how glad they were the place was open. I assume they, like me, needed to be away from the confines of their apartments. Most took a seat, at one of the tables. We started speaking with one another. Started to put words to our thoughts. I was reminded of family wakes I had been to growing up where, because of the tragedy, family members would gather together for food and comfort and support. That's what we all were doing that morning. Complete strangers were coming together. We, and the city, had begun to mourn.

As the days passed, I tried not to isolate myself. I met each day with friends. I went each day to that noontime meeting. There I felt able to talk, to cry, to express anger and grief, confusion and fear. I was grateful I wasn't drinking, because if I had been, I would have numbed with alcohol every feeling I was having. I would have felt nothing, that's true, but I also would have been oblivious to what was happening. I would have been shut down. As extreme and as painful as each day was, following that awful morning, I faced it. I felt it. I'm so glad I did.

One thing I instinctively knew: I had to keep talking about what I had seen and what I was feeling. I saw my therapist every day, whenever he had a free hour. And I would call my parents early each morning during the first few days and cry.

The Handbills

One of the hardest things in those first weeks was passing the countless handbills that were going up all over the city—each with a different face and the bold word MISSING across the top. As the days went on and the number of those postings grew, looking at the word became heart-wrenching, knowing that these faces of strangers, of people loved and worried about, were not merely missing. But, to use any word other than "missing" would be to admit that hope was fading. And, as each day passed into another, the city waited, praying for a miracle recovery of even one lone survivor.

And as the weeks wore on, the handbills seemed to stick to the billboards and buildings and utility poles where they were pasted, with a desperate determination to remain there in spite of the slight tears and rips caused by the wind, the print faded in the sun, the word MISSING running, in the rain, onto the faces of those strangers.

The faces of the "missing" became the faces of "victims." So many, many faces. I found myself wondering if I had passed any of them that morning on my way to work. Had I looked into one of those faces and exchanged a glance or a smile? Did any of those faces belong to the people I saw falling to their deaths? I avoided the areas of the city where I knew there were a lot of handbills. It hurt too much, trying to take in the fact that so many people were gone, that so many had died.

Joe and Judd

On the Friday after the 11th, two 8x10-photocopied pictures of two young men from my apartment building were taped to the glass door leading into our lobby. They had been roommates, friends since middle school. They had worked in the south tower, for the same company, on the same floor. A makeshift memorial was already set up in our lobby: a table with a candle, a vase of flowers, and two bottles of beer.

The two young men had lived in an apartment on the first floor, along with two other friends. I didn't know any of their names. They were just "the frat boys" to me because they were always throwing parties and looked as if they were only just out of college.

One of the roommates was taping pictures of his friends to the wall. I told him how sorry I was and finally learned his and his friends' names. His name was Bert. His friends were Joe and Judd. Bert told me that, after the first plane had hit, one of the guys, I believe it was Judd, had called his girlfriend and said he and Joe were okay, and they were leaving the south tower. That was the last anyone had heard from them.

I can't bear to think of how many spouses, partners, parents, or friends received a call from a loved one that morning, telling them they were okay and were leaving their offices and never came home.

Our apartment building became a close-knit community within those following weeks. Each day, the memorial in our lobby expanded. Arrangements of flowers, with their sweet scents, filled the surrounding floor space. Candles of all shapes and sizes were scattered among the bouquets. Stepping into the lobby from the elevator, one could feel the noticeable rise in temperature from the heat of all those candles, which stayed lit throughout the days and nights. The wall of condolences behind the display was filled with cards and messages from other tenants and with candid photos of Joe and Judd.

As people on the block became aware that two young men from the neighborhood were among those gone, they would pass our building's glass front, stopping to look into our lobby—at the memorial. People would sometimes come in and add their flowers to the others.

I was still getting up early each day, so some mornings I went down to the lobby and, in the predawn quiet, scraped away dried candle wax from the tiled floor and replaced or relit those candles whose flames had gone out. I went to the fruit and vegetable market on our corner and bought fresh flowers to replenish those that were beginning to wilt. I didn't know those two young friends, those two frat boys, Joe and Judd, but I mourned their passing. Grieving them was a way for me to express my grief for all the lives that had been taken that day, thinking particularly of all those young, young men and young women who, as they went to work that morning of the 11th, had their whole lives ahead of them.

A Luncheon

One week following the attack, the employees of the law firm I worked for were called to meet together at a hotel in midtown. It would be a luncheon. More than that, though, it would be a time to face one another, each of us with our own story of that morning.

All of our employees had been accounted for after the 11th, except for one. One of our lawyers. He was a volunteer fireman for the town he lived in, outside of the city. He was last seen running toward the towers, after the first plane had struck, doing what came so naturally to him, trying to help. He was now one of the "missing" and eventually became one of the "victims."

As I arrived at the luncheon, I could see people looking for their coworkers, the person they sat beside each day, the ones they ate lunch with. Our hugs were genuine, but our emotions were kept in place. We had coffee; we mingled, and we made some very, very small talk.

I looked at the faces, the expressions, the forced animation. No one wanted to talk about what we had all experienced just a week ago. We feigned interest in other topics of conversation. Only our eyes held the thoughts we were really thinking, the thoughts that were too difficult to put into words.

I found myself leaning against a wall, isolating myself from the group. I stood there, my mind filling with images of the 11th, as I fought back tears.

Eventually, we were called into the banquet room. It was filled with round tables, set beautifully. A podium, a microphone, and a piano stood on the raised platform in the front. We began finding tables to sit at, idle chatter filling the background. We could no longer dance around the subject at hand. It was the time to address why we were there, time to answer the simple question, "Now what?"

On my seat was a sheet of paper with the words to "America the Beautiful" printed on it.

Someone went to the piano, and we were asked to stand and sing. It was the first patriotic song I had heard, or sung, since the attack. The emotion and significance of the words pierced my heart. Tears could no longer be held back. As I cried, one of our lawyers, someone I didn't really know, came up and held me, and continued to hold me until the song was over.

I forget the order of that afternoon, as I forget many things that have to do with the weeks following the attack. Of course, opening remarks were made. Our missing lawyer was mentioned and given a moment of silence. His brother was introduced. He spoke of his brother—not quite a eulogy, yet his words, the words he used to describe his brother, were all in the past tense.

A husband and wife team of grief counselors spoke to us. The firm had brought them in to provide individual and group counseling. They spoke briefly on what we might expect to go through—trauma, mourning, grief. I heard from them, for the first time, the words "posttraumatic stress syndrome." It would be months before I understood what those words meant.

As they continued talking to us, a secretary broke down, sobbing, and had to be helped out of the room. Lunch was over.

Back To Work

My law firm's office building hadn't been structurally damaged, but it would be weeks before we would be able to go back down to it. Until then, we, like so many other displaced companies, set up temporary offices in a hotel on the East Side in midtown. Most everyone was working there before the second week was over. I couldn't bring myself to go. I called and spoke with my supervisor. I was told to take all the time I needed. I did.

Two or three weeks later, when I started back to work, I found that I could walk to the temporary office from my apartment. It was then that I realized that I had not left the safety of my neighborhood since the 11th and that I was avoiding riding the subway.

Each morning walking there, I would look at the tall buildings as I passed them. I would visualize a plane crashing into them. I would map out my plan if it should happen. I wouldn't run from it. This time I would run toward it.

At work, the events of the morning of September 11th played over and over in my head. I think my mind was still trying to comprehend what it had taken in that day—the sights and sounds and the smells, the stickiness of that stranger's blood on my hands, the taste of burning ashes in the air.

How arbitrary it all had been as to who had died, who had lived. There were the incredible stories of people walking from the rubble, the stories of people who should have been there that morning but weren't, the stories of the people who shouldn't have been down there, but were.

You know, I don't believe I had witnessed the wrath of anyone's God that morning. What I had been a witness to when I looked up at those burning towers was the ultimate evil that man is capable of. The evidence of just how deep hatred could run, how far it could go.

But I had also been a witness to something else that day—down on the ground. I witnessed the ultimate goodness of man, the evidence of how strong courage could be, to what lengths it would go.

I believe God was in the hands of everyone who reached out to help someone else. He was in the arms of people on the streets as they embraced one another. He was in the tears of strangers who cried together. He was in all the lives that were given in the line of duty, in the acts of heroism. He was in the hearts of the people across the country who, as they watched the horror from afar, felt compassion.

My Apartment

A few weeks later, I looked around my studio apartment and saw that it looked like a disaster area. By then, I had started buying newspapers, and each day's issue was strewn about the floor, as were plastic Coke bottles. Empty coffee cups from the deli remained on whatever surface space had been near me when I finished drinking them. The brown bags they had been put into lay crumpled on the floor, as did discarded clothes. Dishes rose in a pile in the sink; trash cans overflowed.

There had been a subconscious design to this disarray. I had created a personal sanctum, a place that held near me the devastating effect of the morning of the 11th, a place where the elements of that horrific morning were still real.

As a gesture to myself and to the awareness that I couldn't continue living like that, I slowly started the process of picking up or throwing away the wreckage I had found consolation in. Bit by bit, day by day, newspapers were taken out, coffee cups and paper bags thrown away, clothes picked up.

Two things remained where I had dropped them the afternoon of the 11th: the pants and shoes I had been wearing when I went to work that morning. The shoes, a pair of brown loafers that had been polished to a solid shine and that had still looked like new, were now scuffed and scraped to a degree that no amount of polish could conceal.

The pair of pants I had been wearing was intact, except for a slight tear on one of the legs and a few black marks. I couldn't believe that there wasn't any blood on them, particularly when I had knelt down to help that injured man. I knew that I would never wear those pants again—or the pair of shoes. Weirdly, the shirt I had been wearing I had put in the dirty clothes basket when I took it off, and forgot all about it. But the shoes and pants, I regarded as souvenirs of what I lived through.

I took a 9x12 FedEx box, which was among the trash that had accumulated, and ceremoniously placed the shoes inside. I took the pants and put them atop the shoes. I closed the box and placed it on the top shelf of my closet, knowing that, at least for now, I planned on keeping these clothes with me forever. I didn't think I would ever want to look at them again. But, for whatever the reason, I just couldn't throw them away. They represented too much to me. They were the only physical reminders of my place in that day. If, years from now, my memories became hazy, my feelings detached, I could take the box from wherever it would be at that time, open it, and be able to touch, to feel, to remember that morning.

"Ground Zero"

I didn't want to go back downtown, back to what was now being called "Ground Zero." I was already down there every day in my mind. But eventually the time came when the office building downtown was ready, and we were scheduled to return, and, simply put, I didn't want fear to be my reason for not returning.

Because I wasn't sure how I would react, on November 10th, the Saturday before we were to return, I decided to go down to Ground Zero…by myself. It was early, around 7 a.m. It was another beautiful day. I stood on the corner of Broadway and Fulton, outside my office building. Looking at Building Number 5 World Trade Center or, rather, the blackened, charred remains of it, I did what came so naturally those days. I started crying.

I had my head down, and I felt an arm go around my shoulders. I looked up, and it was a policeman. He tightened his hold on me and said, "Let it out." I put my head on his shoulder and wept. Another officer came up to us, and as I composed myself, they talked with me. I told them about my personal experience of that day. They both were incredibly consoling, and I felt very comfortable with them—comfortable enough to ask if they might let me into Ground Zero, to stand where I had been the morning of the 11th. One of them went to speak with his superior and then came back and said, "Just follow us."

The two officers led me through security, and through the barriers, and we stepped out onto Church Street, the street I had been on during most of the attack—the street where I had watched all those people fall to their deaths—the street I was on when the second plane hit—the street from which I had to run for my life.

I felt that being able to stand there now was a gift—a gift to be able to acknowledge, honor, and show my respect to all those courageous victims. Standing there, I thought about and accepted having been a part of that day. I took in the whole scope of the site. Only a small segment of the façade of the north tower remained standing, the tower I had tried to run to, wanting to do something. I told the officers about that and pointed out to them where I had to turn back. They assured me I had probably saved my own life by doing that.

We stayed about 15–20 minutes. When it was time to go, I asked for just a moment alone, and they graciously stepped back a bit. I took my final moment with the site, with the spirits of those who had died, with the gratitude that I was alive. I had brought six roses with me. I laid them down, knowing they wouldn't remain there long. But for that moment, I had contributed something beautiful to that place of tragedy and loss. It was enough.

Past security and back out on the corner of Broadway and Fulton, the officers and I said our good-byes, and they stuck out their hands to shake mine. I, instead, hugged each of them and told them that I considered them my angels that morning. Two angels in blue.

I left them and walked back to the subway, to the Chambers Street entrance, crying again, but now I cried with a serenity and feeling of gratitude toward God, the world, the universe for the gift of having just stood on hallowed ground.

November 12th

That next Monday, November 12th, we started working back at our building. November 12th, two months and one day since the terrorist attack. November 12th, the morning Flight 587 crashed in Queens.

As soon as we received the first inner-office e-mail, that morning, about the crash of Flight 587, I realized that life was no longer as it had been on September 10th. As everyone waited for further developments about the crash, it seemed so strange to be hoping it had been an accident.

All the fears, all the feelings we had been experiencing for the past two months were rekindled. Television carried familiar images of burning debris, rescue workers carrying draped corpses, firefighters and police staggering out of the devastation, gasping for air. It brought it all back.

Each morning as I arrived at Chambers Street, the smell of smoke was present as soon as the doors of the subway cars opened.

Coming up onto the street, the smell was even stronger above ground. Barricades now blocked certain streets. Walking toward Ground Zero, the number of policemen/women, the soldiers in uniform, and the sight of guns suggested a military state, a city torn by war.

St. Paul's Church, next to my office building, was being used as a relief center for those protecting the sacred site and for those who worked among the ruins of what was now a huge burial ground. St. Paul's had become an improvised memorial to those who were gone. The high, black, wrought-iron fence in front of the church was adorned with tributes—a huge card made by a grade school class in the Midwest, photos of victims, sheets draped across the fence and covered with the signatures and messages of condolence from those who came by. Flowers, candles, personal mementoes left behind.

Early in the morning, crowds would start to gather, to stand in silence, to see for themselves, to try and take it in. But I winced each time I saw a camera being held up.

I labeled all those who gathered from early morning to early evening as tourists, there only to gawk and stare at something that I felt the need to protect. I wanted to yell at them, the parents with their children, the young kids pointing and staring, "This isn't just some tourist attraction. You have no idea what really happened here." I know now that I used them as an outlet for the anger that was inside me. A pent-up anger that needed to be directed at someone, anyone. Not until I took my own parents there did I realize the significance and importance for others to visit the site.

Thanksgiving

My folks came into the city to be with me on Thanksgiving. I would usually have spent it at their home in Pennsylvania or at my sister's in Maryland, the whole family together. But this year, I was part of a much larger family. I belonged to this city, and we had just suffered a terrible loss. I couldn't leave it. To do so would have been like deserting my blood family after the loss of a loved one. I didn't think I would want to be with anyone that Thanksgiving. I thought I'd prefer to be alone, not knowing what the day or the city would be like for me. But my parents, being parents and sometimes knowing better than I, drove in to be with me, just for the day.

When they arrived very early Thanksgiving day, I asked them if they wanted to go to Ground Zero. Though they had their hesitations about whether to go or not, they did feel it was important to see it. And I found it was important for me to show it to them.

We took a cab down. The crowds were already in place, even by early morning, on a holiday. I could see, from my parents' expressions as we got out of the cab, that they were already taken aback by what they saw. We walked to St. Paul's, next to my building, to the, now even busier, relief center. I stood back and let them take it in on their own.

I watched my dad sign one of the sheets hanging there, putting his own private thoughts down in words. As I watched him, my mom came over to me, tears in her eyes, and simply said, "This is so sad."

I walked them to one of the barricades and pointed out to them what had happened and where I had been. My hands shook, my voice trembled. A woman next to us looked at me. One of my parents told her I had been there that day. The woman reached over and took my hand.

We had our Thanksgiving dinner that afternoon at a diner in my neighborhood. We each had the turkey special. It was a lot of food. It was a Thanksgiving I will never forget.

My Own Leap

Workday after workday, I passed the burned-out shell of Building Number 5, the building where my favorite bookstore had been. I would feel apprehension flood me as I emerged onto the streets from the subway each morning. When the weekend of that first week back finally came, I felt emotionally spent, depleted, drained. I think I slept most of Saturday and Sunday.

And now, each day down there was a sad reminder of what was no longer there, of what was gone. I no longer enjoyed going downtown each morning. Lunchtime was particularly difficult. I would go outside, quickly buy something, and rush back inside to eat. I couldn't even bear to look toward where I had sat so many noontimes. There was no more plaza, no fountain, no golden sphere. All that was there now was smoking debris, pieces of equipment and burned-out remains.

I was able to do my job efficiently each day. My coworkers and I were able to laugh and make an occasional joke. We talked about other things than just that day. If anything, it seemed we tried to avoid talking about it.

Yet, as I sat behind my computer each day, I couldn't stop thinking of all who had died on the 11th, nor did I want to stop thinking of them.

Their deaths had caused me to look at my life. And what I was seeing was a life that had been defined by a job that I had let determine who I was and what I did. Aside from having faced the fears I had about coming back downtown, I also had to face the fears that had prevented me from living my life for so many years.

And I did.

On the Monday of my third week back at work, the week after Thanksgiving, I gave my notice. That coming Friday would be my last day. I had decided to walk away from a job I had for 13 years, a job I never planned on making a career, a job I settled into, with the security of good money, great benefits, and paid vacation, making it too easy not to leave. But, it certainly hadn't been a job that had fulfilled me. It hadn't been a job that provided any outlet for creativity. It hadn't been a job I really wanted to do. It had just been a job.

A job that, when I started, was only going to be for a year or two, while I decided what to do next with my life. That year or two became 13 years so quickly and easily. And I had forgotten all about deciding.

Life and my perspective of it changed the moment I walked through that revolving door on September 11th.

I saw many people lose their lives that morning. In particular, I think of the many people I saw jump to their deaths. I think of their courage, knowing they were going to die. I think of that one moment in which they each had to decide for themselves how their lives were going to end. They had to choose how to die. They took that leap.

And I'm one of the lucky ones. I'm still here, and now I had to choose how to live. I owed it to myself and to their memories to do just that. To take my own leap.

I didn't want another number of years to go by and find myself asking "what if?" I'd asked myself that question too many times already during my life.

My life had, at one time, become a rut, a routine. And now I found that I had fallen into another one.

I didn't know what I would do after I quit. The past couple of years, I'd taken to heart the motto "one day at a time." I now had a whole new appreciation for those practical words.

I began writing about my experience of 9/11. Mostly for myself. I also sent e-mails to friends and family at the time. I was encouraged by many to keep writing. And I have.

And life has continued one day at a time.

The rescue and recovery ended, as it had to. Ground Zero no longer holds any physical evidence of what took place there. It's now just a huge, stark, vacant pit, waiting for the reconstruction to begin.

The sphere that sat atop the fountain in the plaza was amazingly found in all the rubble, though in pieces. It was lovingly put back together by the workers at the site and now stands in Battery Park; once again whole, though dented and damaged, but standing strong. Much like our city.

There is a thin veil of disbelief I sometimes try to wrap myself in. A covering of resistance to the harsh truth. A slight remaining ache that wants to deny in the face of all evidence that day in September ever happened.

Yet, the reality is…I think of 9/11 every day.

I still tense when I hear an airplane overhead and automatically look up to see if it's flying too low.

Now, whenever I hear a siren, I hear, in my mind, the loud wailing of all those sirens that day.

At the most unexpected moments, images of that day run through my mind like a newsreel.

I have an occasional flashback where something stimulates my whole body and, for a brief second or two, I'm back there—in that day—amid the falling debris.

I continue to have nightmares occasionally, and sometimes I feel the need to sleep with a light on, as I did the first few weeks after the 11th.

I think often about the man with the split skull. I want to believe he survived his injury, but I know that, in actuality, he probably didn't.

I wonder, too, about the fate of my "coffee man." His cart was on a corner right across from Building Number 5.

And the woman who lost her shoe. What about her?

Every cliché about living for today now seems like the greatest wisdom.

During my limited lifetime, I've learned to accept, and not be ashamed of, who I am. I've learned to admit being powerless over some things. I've learned I don't have to regret my past, or shut the door on it. I've learned to ask for help—from others and from whatever higher power there is beyond myself.

And now as I learn to live for today:

I will remember all the goodness that we are capable of, that we displayed to ourselves and to the world.

I will know what it means to show courage when I think of the men and women who died—while trying to help others live.

I will know that only through feeling can healing begin.

I will believe that those who are gone would encourage us to live.

I will trust that they are smiling down on us as we each try the best we can to do just that.

No, I will not forget what I lived through, what we all lived through, that day in September.

And to honor those who are gone, I will not forget to live.

About the Author

ARTIE VAN WHY, originally from a small town in Montgomery County, Maryland, lived in New York City over twenty-five years, pursuing a stage career.

Artie left show business in 1988 and entered the corporate world. He worked for the same law firm in midtown Manhattan for thirteen years. In June of 2001, his firm moved to other quarters downtown, across from the World Trade Center. He was at work the morning of September 11th and witnessed the horror of that day from the streets. Artie eventually quit his job after returning to work for three weeks back at his office's building near what was now called Ground Zero. He began writing about his experience of that day and the days and weeks following, giving a vivid account of what it was like to be in New York City. He sent some of his writings to friends and family via e-mails, and they, in turn, forwarded them to their friends and families. In a short period of time, people across the country were reading Artie's e-mails. He began receiving e-mails from people expressing their gratitude in being given a glimpse of what it was like to be in New York City during that time. He was encouraged to keep writing, and he did. Led by a personal conviction that this was what he should do, Artie decided to put his writing into script form. Laboring over draft after draft, Artie wanted to create a work he could share with people across the country.

He met famed actor, Richard Masur, through a mutual friend. Richard had done weeks of volunteer work at Ground Zero during the weeks of rescue and recovery. With Richard's help, Artie put the final touches on the script and produced a staged reading of what was now a one-man play called *That Day In September* in New York City. The reading was a success, a sold-out evening. With Richard Masur now involved as director, the first mounted production of *That Day In September* premiered on the campus of California Lutheran University, in Thousand Oaks, California, shortly after the one-year anniversary of September 11th. The play then moved to the Celebration Theater in Los Angeles, where it opened to critical acclaim.

Back in New York, Artie mounted a workshop production of *That Day In September*, in preparation for a New York run. In August of 2003, *That Day In September* opened Off Broadway for a limited run.

After the New York production, Artie moved to Lancaster County, in Pennsylvania, where he still resides.